HOW IT WAS

THE ROMANS IN BRITAIN

Dorothy Metcalf

B.T. Batsford Ltd, London

CONTENTS

© Dorothy Metcalf 1993

First published 1993

Typeset by Goodfellow & Egan, Cambridge
and printed in Hong Kong

Published by
B. T. Batsford Ltd
4 Fitzhardinge Street
London W1H 0AH

A CIP catalogue record for this book is available from the British Library

ISBN 0 7134 6575 1

Thanks go to the *How It Was* series editors for advice and editorial input: Madeline Jones, Jessica Saraga and Michael Rawcliffe; also to Sarah Vernon-Hunt for her particularly helpful suggestions.

Frontispiece: *A statue from the second century AD showing the Emperor Hadrian with his left foot on a slain barbarian.*

Cover illustration: *A reconstruction by Alan Sorrell of a fourth century bastion, reproduced by permission of the Museum of London.*

INTRODUCTION

The Romans ruled Britain for three hundred and fifty years, approximately the same length of time from the execution of King Charles I to the present day. According to legend, Rome was founded in 753 BC by Romulus and Remus, twins who were left to die, but who were then found and brought up by a wolf. The city quickly grew and by 140 BC a huge empire had been established around the Mediterranean Sea. In 55 BC Julius Caesar, after conquering Gaul (now France), decided to invade Britain. He was unsuccessful despite two attempts but a hundred years later, in 43 AD, Britain was conquered, and for the first time came under foreign rule.

The Romans brought many changes to British life. Most important of all, there was now a very large army of occupation, spread over most of Britain and Wales and into Scotland. This was a powerful army: tens of thousands of highly-trained soldiers with advanced weapons, all speaking a different language, Latin, and with many different customs. Inevitably, the influence of tribal chieftains who had previously ruled became very much less and new methods of government and taxation were introduced.

The face of Britain changed too. For the first time towns were built, with public buildings, houses, shops, workshops, temples (the picture on the right shows the London basilica), and sometimes public baths, theatres, and amphitheatres. The more luxurious houses even had central heating and running water. A network of wide, well-maintained roads was constructed across the country, along which armies and people and goods could travel easily and in safety. There was greatly increased trade with the rest of Europe, and many more foods and luxury objects were brought here. Industries and farming flourished. People learned to read and write, and different religions took root.

It would be good to think that all this meant that the majority of British people lived longer and led happier lives. Sadly, what evidence we have from the inscriptions in tombstones and the study of skeletons would suggest that if they survived infancy, people's life expectancy was very short, perhaps as low as fifty for men and forty for women.

And what did they think of their conquerors? Some British women married soldiers, and numbers of Romans stayed in Britain after they had been discharged from the army. But probably the most important piece of evidence as to how they felt is the size of the army the Romans kept here. The very great number of soldiers stationed in Britain suggests that *pax Romana* (Roman peace) was never to be taken for granted.

A reconstruction of the Roman basilica in London.

Introductory Quiz

Do you know?

What the Romans hoped to find in Britain?

Which cosmetic was made from the sweat of sheep's wool?

Whether the Romans used soap?

How a Roman soldier was rewarded for being the first over the wall in a siege?

Why gladiators were usually either criminals or prisoners of war?

THE ROMAN INVASION

Why did the Romans come to Britain? They had already conquered much of Europe and North Africa. The geographer Strabo, who lived at about the same time (c. 64 BC – AD 19), tells us that they came for corn, cattle, gold, silver and iron, hides, slaves and clever hunting dogs. Julius Caesar, the Roman general, who led the first invasion, wrote that in almost all the Gallic campaigns the Gauls had received reinforcements from the Britons (Gaul was the name of much of present-day France). He also said that it would be a great advantage to visit the island to see what its inhabitants were like.

The landing in Kent in 55 BC was not a Roman success. The Britons fought hard, and when a sudden storm and an exceptionally high tide led to the sinking of many of Caesar's ships, he was forced to withdraw to Gaul.

The following year Caesar set sail with a much bigger fleet of more than 800 ships, and this time he made more progress. One of the main reasons for his advance was that at that time Britain was not a united country. It was divided into tribal territories, each with its own chieftain, and tribes were often at war with each other. The Romans exploited this and were able to push on as far as where Bedfordshire, Buckinghamshire and Hertfordshire are today. At this point they decided to go no further, and after hostages had been taken and an annual tax, called a *tribute*, was agreed upon, Caesar and his army returned to Gaul.

A map of the Roman empire at its height in the second century AD. Why do you think the empire expanded around the Mediterranean rather than north into what is now Germany?

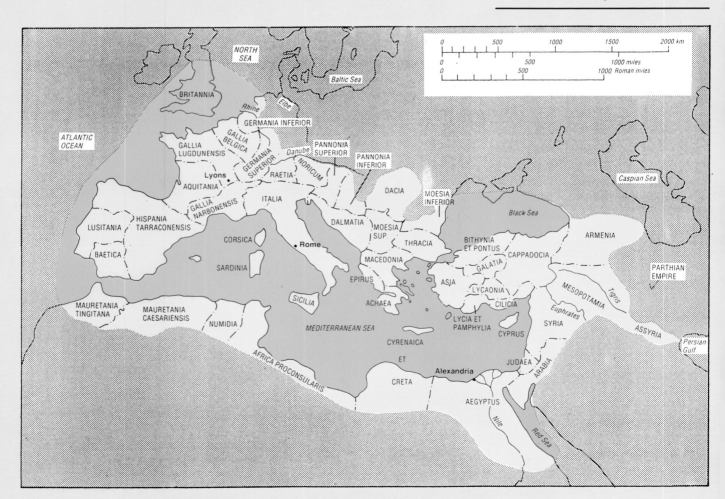

It was almost a hundred years before the Romans returned. In 27 BC an invasion was called off because there was war in Gaul, and later the Emperor Augustus said that no more territory should be annexed. The Emperor Claudius, however, thought that a military victory would make himself more popular with the people, and in 43 AD he gave the order to invade Britain again.

About 50,000 men under Aulus Plautius landed on the Kent coast, and marched swiftly inland. The British tribes who opposed him were heavily defeated and retreated to the Thames. Claudius himself then arrived in Britain with some elephants, more troops, and the Praetorian Guard, his personal bodyguard. Near Colchester a number of smaller tribes surrendered to him, but after only a fortnight he returned to Rome. An arch was built to commemorate the defeat of the Britons and Claudius himself received a *triumph*, a victory procession, which was a very great honour.

Back in Britain, Aulus Plautius divided the army into three main divisions. One was sent towards what is now Leicester and the midlands, one north towards Lincoln and one west. There is evidence of fierce resistance. One Roman general, Vespasian, according to his biographer Suetonius, fought more than thirty battles. Nevertheless, within four years Aulus Plautius had established a frontier from Lyme Bay to the Humber, and the Romans dominated the whole of central and southern Britain. They were to remain in Britain for over three hundred and fifty years.

A statue of Julius Caesar, who led the first invasion of Britain in 55 AD.

THE ROMAN INVASION

Warfare

The following extract is from the only history written by a great Roman general about his own campaigns. Here Julius Caesar writes about the conquest of Britain.

The natives, on realizing his intention, had sent forward their cavalry and a number of chariots, which they are accustomed to use in warfare: the rest of their troops followed close behind and were ready to oppose the landing. The Romans were faced with great difficulties. The size of the ships made it impossible to run them aground except in fairly deep water; and soldiers, unfamiliar with the ground, with their hands full, and weighted down by the heavy burden of their arms, had at the same time to jump down from the ships, get a footing in the waves, and fight the enemy, who, standing on dry land or advancing only a short way into the water, fought with all their limbs unencumbered, and on perfectly familiar ground, boldly hurling javelins, and galloping their horses, which were trained in this kind of work.

(From Julius Caesar, *The Conquest of Gaul*)

Q

The Romans were faced with grave difficulties in trying to land. Why do you think they succeeded in the end?

CHECK YOUR UNDERSTANDING

Can you remember the meaning of the following?

Annex
Commemorate
Praetorian guard
Tribute
Triumph

THINGS TO DO

1 55 BC means 55 years before Christ was born. 43 AD means 43 years after Christ was born (AD stand for *anno domini*, which is the Latin for 'in the year of the Lord'). What is the year after 54 BC? Exactly how many years are there between 54 BC and 43 AD?
2 Can you discover why the Romans would know less about tides than the Britons?
3 Find on a map the places the Romans reached on their expeditions: Buckinghamshire, Bedfordshire and Hertfordshire in 54 BC, and Lyme Bay (on the south coast) and the River Humber in 47 AD.

Maiden castle in Dorset, a very large Iron Age fort that continued to be inhabited throughout the Roman occupation period. Some archaeologists believe that it was the scene of a fierce battle between Britons and the invading Roman army.

CAN YOU REMEMBER ?

There were three main reasons why the Romans came to Britain. What were they?
Why did the invasion of 55 BC fail?
Who commanded the 54 BC expedition, and what was the name of the Emperor who decided to invade in 43 AD?
What were the things that Strabo said the Romans would find in Britain?

Roman Victory

In this passage, Tacitus, writing in about 113 AD, describes how the Roman army fought. He is describing the battle in 51 AD between the British chieftain Caratacus and the Roman general Ostorius.

> The Roman general was . . . alarmed by the obstacle of the river, the rampart that had been built, the overhanging crags and numbers of fierce warriors. But his soldiers demanded the right to fight . . . Ostorius . . . led his enthusiastic soldiers forward across the river. At the rampart both sides hurled their javelins, and we suffered the heavier casualties in killed and wounded. Our men locked their shields over their heads to form a 'tortoise', broke down the rough barricade, set to work with their swords on equal terms, and drove the natives to the hilltops. Close behind them ran our men, the light-armed auxiliaries attacking with their spears, the legions in close order. The British lines were thrown into confusion, for they had no helmets or breast plates to protect them. If they stood up to the auxiliaries, the legionaires' swords and javelins cut them down; if they faced the legions they fell to the broadswords and spears of the auxiliaries.

(From Tacitus, *Annals*)

Tacitus wrote this fifty years after the battle actually happened. Where would he have got his information? Can we trust his version entirely?

The Emperor Claudius, who reigned 41–54 AD. It was Claudius who ordered the conquest of Britain. He was poisoned by his fourth wife Agrippina who wanted her son by a previous marriage to be emperor. The son's name was Nero – find out what you can about this colourful emperor.

'She was a huge woman, with a piercing glance and a strident voice: a mass of chestnut hair hung below her waist. Round her neck was a great golden *torque* (necklace). She wore a full, flowing, tartan dress, and over it a thick cloak, fastened by a brooch . . . On this occasion she grasped a spear to terrify everyone'.

This is how Cassius Dio, a historian, described Boudica, queen of the Iceni tribe, who in 60 AD led a major revolt against the Romans. When her husband died, the Romans attempted to take over Iceni territory, in what is now East Anglia. With the neighbouring Trinovantes as allies, Boudica put the Romans to flight, and Colchester, London and St. Albans were all badly damaged. Another Roman historian, Tacitus, tells us that it was the discipline and superior weaponry of the Romans that in the end defeated Boudica, and that 80,000 Britons were killed in the final battle. Boudica is supposed to have poisoned herself.

Another serious rebellion took place in the north at the beginning of the second century, and it was after this that Hadrian's Wall was built. Although only parts of it remain, the wall is still one of the most important legacies of Roman rule. The Emperor Hadrian came to Britain in 122 AD and instead of defending the north with scattered forts, decided to build this huge, fortified barrier.

The wall, built between 122 AD and 128 AD, was 128 kilometres long and stretched from Newcastle to Bowness. It was built of stone and was 2.5 to 3 metres thick and 4.5 metres high for most of its length. Along it at intervals of a Roman mile (1481 metres) were forts, big enough for fifty men. Small look-out posts were constructed every 800 metres, and at equal intervals along its entire length, sixteen larger castles each of which could house 1000 men. Behind the wall was a road, and behind that a ditch, 6.5 metres wide and 2.5 metres deep to protect the Romans from attack to the rear.

Settlements grew up outside the forts to house the families of soldiers. If you can, visit Housesteads or Corbridge, where there are fascinating archaeological remains, and collections of objects which show us a little of what life was like 'along the wall'.

When Hadrian died the next emperor, Antoninus, decided to occupy lowland Scotland, and he built another wall 60 kilometres long between the Firth and the Clyde as a new frontier. This wall had no castles and the nineteen forts and three smaller ones were much closer together. The barrier itself was made of turf with a massive ditch in front, and although some stone was used in the construction of the forts, the whole structure was not nearly as solidly built as Hadrian's Wall.

This frontier at the Antonine Wall was held for only a relatively short time. Tribes in southern Scotland were not prepared to accept Roman rule, and constant fighting was a severe drain on Roman manpower. By about 163 AD the Romans were forced to draw back, and Hadrian's Wall was again the accepted frontier.

Hadrian's Wall. The photograph shows dramatically how the wall snaked its way across Britain – even if it meant building it across difficult terrain. How do you think the Romans managed to gather all the materials necessary to build the wall?

CONQUEST

Hadrian's Wall

Imagine moving an estimated two million tons of rock and soil to build the wall and its forts, without the use of modern equipment. The sixteen larger forts built at regular intervals along the length of Hadrian's Wall were all of considerable size with thick stone walls. The one at Housesteads is 200 metres by 100 metres, and like the others could have housed a thousand men. Most of the forts the Romans built were constructed to the same careful design.

The commander's quarters were in the centre in an area called the *praetorium*, with the armoury containing weapons and armour close by. At the back was an open area, where the soldiers could train and exercise, and beside it the *quaestorium*, or paymaster's office. Barracks were built in large blocks around the inside of the walls. The granaries (the food stores) were situated in the middle of the forts.

The mile forts were very much smaller, built for only fifty men, and they housed the sentries who patrolled the walls (a Roman mile was 1481 metres). These mile-castles, as they are sometimes called, were often constructed not in stone, but in timber or turf. Between each of them were two small turrets, built of stone, which were used as signal stations. From other parts of the Roman world we know that the Romans used flags and a semaphore system for signalling as well as beacons and torches.

The Barbarian British

We think of Boudica and her army as defenders of British independence. The Romans thought differently as Tacitus in the *Annals* explains:

> The same massacre took place at the city of Verulamium, [St. Albans today] for the barbarian British, happiest when looting and unenthusiastic about real effort, bypassed the forts and the garrisons, and headed for the spots where they knew the most undefended booty lay. Something like 70,000 Roman citizens and other friends of Rome died in the places I have mentioned. The Britons took no prisoners, sold no captives as slaves, and went in for none of the usual trading of war. They wasted no time in getting down to the bloody business of hanging, burning and crucifying. It was as if they feared that retribution might catch up with them, while their vengeance was only half-complete.
>
> (From Tacitus, *Annals*)

Tacitus speaks of the British killing 70,000 supporters of Rome, and of the Romans killing 80,000 Britons. These figures may not be accurate. Why not?

Why were the armouries and granaries to be found in the centre of forts?

THINGS TO DO

1 Hadrian was very fond of building. Try to find out the name of a town in another part of the Empire built by him. What famous monument did he build in Rome? You should find out these answers in an encyclopaedia.

2 Write an account of a day in the life of a soldier stationed on the Wall.
3 Find on a map Newcastle and Bowness, the places at either end of Hadrian's Wall. Why do you think he decided to build there, and not somewhere else?

The statue of Boudica on Westminster Bridge in London – look especially at the chariot.

CAN YOU REMEMBER ?

Why did the Romans attack the Iceni?
What was the Emperor Hadrian's main reason for building the Wall?
Where was it, and how long was it?
Where was the Antonine Wall? Can you give one reason why it did not remain as a frontier for very long?

CHECK YOUR UNDERSTANDING

Can you remember the meaning of the following words?

Discipline
Garrisoning
Strident
Torque
Turf

An Expensive Mistake?

Sadly, for the Romans, the Walls did not bring lasting peace to the north. Here is Cassius Dio writing c.220 AD about the British and the campaign of the Emperor Severus, who died in York in 211 AD.

> There are two very big tribes in Britain, the Caledonians and the Maeatae . . . The Maeatae live near the cross-wall, which cuts the island in two, and the Caledonians behind them . . . They fight with chariots, with small, fast horses . . . They have shields and short spears, which have bronze knobs on the butt-ends – they bang these on their shields to frighten their enemies – and they also have daggers. They can endure cold and hunger, and any kind of hardship. They hide in their marshes, and hold out for days with only their heads above water. In the woods they live on the bark or roots of trees; for emergencies they prepare a certain kind of food, and if they eat a piece of this the size of a bean, they feel neither hunger or thirst . . . So Severus invaded Caledonia, and met countless troubles doing so . . . Our men suffered terribly in the water, and were attacked wherever they were scattered. Then, being unable to march, they were killed by their comrades to save them from capture, and casualties reached nearly 50,000.

(From Dio, *Roman History*)

It was soon after the events described here that Severus died. He had two sons and his last words to them were 'Stick together, spend your money on the troops, and let everyone else go hang'. They didn't follow his advice; the elder, Caracalla, had his younger brother executed.

Details of the campaign are scanty, but as Britain remained within the Empire, it must have been successful.

THE ROMAN ARMY

The Roman army was a very large, highly-trained, well-equipped fighting force. It was made up of *legions*, each consisting of 5000 men. Every legion was divided into ten *cohorts*, and the cohorts were divided again into *centuries*, which despite their name, consisted of eighty men under the command of *centurions*. Attached to each legion was a medical corps, and about one hundred and twenty horsemen, who acted as scouts and despatch carriers. Many of the legionaries were skilled craftsmen, such as masons or engineers. The emblem of the legion, an eagle, was carried by a legionary wearing a headdress made from either a leopard's or a lion's skin.

At first, only Romans were allowed to join the army, but later men from other countries were allowed to enlist, and were called *auxiliaries*. Slaves were never eligible. Every soldier took an oath of loyalty to the emperor. He had to be strong and healthy, 1.7 metres tall, and be able to speak Latin. A centurion had to be able to read and write. In general, soldiers did not serve in their own countries, and very often after twenty-five years of

service without seeing their homes, they settled in the province where they had been stationed, with a generous sum of money and sometimes a grant of land as well.

Training was hard. Recruits drilled with 23 kilogram packs on their backs, and experienced soldiers were kept fit by frequent marches, manoeuvres, and fort-building exercises. Discipline was strict: centurions carried canes that were freely used. *Decimation*, the execution of every tenth man in a unit, was the punishment for cowardice. The punishment considered the worst of all and given for shameful defeat in battle, was the disbanding of the entire legion.

Legionaries wore leather tunics, strong boots and when it was cold, leggings and woollen cloaks. They had helmets and breastplates, and carried shields. Their weapons were a javelin, a short sword and a dagger. Centurions had leg armour called *greaves*, their helmets had plumes, and they wore red cloaks that could be easily seen. The cost of uniforms, weapons and food was deducted from a soldier's pay, and he probably ended up with about a fifth of what he earned.

There were also larger weapons. A *ballista* was like a huge crossbow. It was mounted on a cart, usually pulled by ten men, and it could fire stones or iron bolts that could kill at a range of 400 metres. An *onager*, a kind of massive catapult, could hurl bigger stones 200 metres. A device for protection was the *tortoise*, the locking together of shields over soldiers' heads.

The highest honour for a general was a *triumph*, a victory procession through the streets of Rome. Individual soldiers could be awarded armlets, medals and crowns. The highest award was a crown of gold, given to the first man over the wall in a siege.

*The modern Ermine Street Guard (named after the road that ran from York (*Eboracum*) to London (*Londinium*) in Roman times) show what it would have been like to face a charge by a Roman unit. Can you tell the individual rank and position of each soldier from what they are carrying?*

THE ROMAN ARMY

Trajan's Column

Trajan's column was built in Rome to celebrate the victories of the Emperor Trajan. On it are sculpted the story of his campaigns like a gigantic spiral strip cartoon, and these pictures are an invaluable source of information about the Roman army of the time. There is a plaster model of the column in the Victoria and Albert Museum in London. At what point in a siege might the legionaries shown below form a tortoise (see Glossary)? What would be a major disadvantage of a tortoise?

Roman ships

Caesar described the new ships built for the 54 BC invasion of Britain. There is a ship depicted on the coin shown on p. 26.

To enable them to be loaded quickly and beached easily he had them made slightly lower than those which we generally use in the Mediterranean . . . To enable them, however, to carry a heavy cargo, including a large number of animals, they were made somewhat wider than the ships we use in other waters. They were all to be of a type suitable for both sailing and rowing.

(From Julius Caesar, *The Conquest of Gaul*)

What animals would be needed by the Roman army?

CHECK YOUR UNDERSTANDING

Can you remember the meaning of the following words?

Auxiliaries
Ballista
Decimate
Greaves
Onager

There are 2,500 figures sculpted into Trajan's column and they tell us a great deal about the Roman army. What are the soldiers doing in the scenes depicted here?

CAN YOU REMEMBER?

What was the emblem of a legion? Who carried it, and what did he wear?
How do we know that discipline was very strict?
Why might one think, wrongly, that a century consisted of a hundred men?
Before you could join the Roman army, what conditions did you have to fulfil?

THINGS TO DO

1 Find out what you can about conditions of service in the British Army today. In what ways have things changed for the common soldier?

2 Study the picture of the legionaries opposite. What weapons are they carrying? What do you think each might be used for?

3 Imagine you are an auxiliary from Spain serving in Britain. Write an account of how you feel about living in Britain.

Setting Up Camp

Here is a description of a Roman army camp, written by a Jewish priest Josephus in 75 AD.

Whenever they invade enemy country, they never engage in battle till they have fortified a camp. They do not build in any vague or random fashion . . . If the ground is uneven they level it. The encampment is marked out as a square . . . The interior is divided into rows of tents: from the outside the perimeter looks like a wall, and towers are spaced out at regular intervals. Between the towers they put various artillery machines for firing stones or arrows. Four gates are built into this surrounding rampart, one in each side: they provide an easy entrance for the baggage-animals, and are wide enough for the troops to dash out on quick raids in emergencies . . . If necessary, a ditch is dug round outside the wall, six feet deep and six feet wide . . . When camp is struck the trumpet sounds, and every man springs to his duty . . . The announcer asks three times in their native language, if they are ready for war. They three times shout loudly and enthusiastically, 'Ready', raising their right hands in the air. They then set off, all marching silently and in good order. Lots are drawn for the legion that is to head the column.

(From Josephus, *The Jewish War*)

Often, when the legions left camp and did not intend to return, the camp was set on fire. Why was this?

Before the Romans came most Britons lived either in settlements or in hillforts. One of the most important changes the Romans made was the building of towns. Towns could provide services for the army, and better markets for everyone. They were easier to defend, taxes could be collected, and laws enforced more effectively there.

The first new town, Colchester, was built in 49 AD as a settlement for retired army veterans, and later Lincoln and Gloucester were founded for the same reason. St. Albans had always been a tribal centre, and by 60 AD it had a well-laid out street system, a thriving market, and good defences. London, too, was enlarged by the Romans and was described by Tacitus, a Roman historian, as important for business and merchandise. Within fifty years of the invasion there were several more towns, amongst them Canterbury, Exeter, Winchester and Leicester. Altogether under Roman rule at least a hundred towns were built.

Most of them grew up in a fairly haphazard fashion to supply the needs of the army, but the more important ones were very carefully planned on a grid system with roads between 5 and 8 metres wide. At first, towns in peaceful provinces had no walls, but by 400 AD every town had them. There were usually four main gateways. Outside would be the cemetery, the *aqueduct*, which carried the town's water supply, and the *amphitheatre*.

In the centre of the town was the *forum*, a large open space, often entered through a handsome gateway, such as at Silchester. On three sides were shops and stalls, and on the fourth the *basilica*, the most important building of all, which contained a hall, the room where the town council met, the law courts, the *tabularium* where official records and documents were kept, and the treasury.

Shops, workshops and taverns lined the main streets. There would be barracks for soldiers near the gates, temples for religious worship, and inns for travellers.

Many towns had public baths, and those at Bath remain in the best condition. They were similar to modern Turkish baths, with cold, warm and hot rooms, and people went there to meet their friends as well as to bathe. At the Wroxeter baths there was an outdoor swimming pool and an exercise hall too.

We know of three theatres, at Colchester, Canterbury and St. Albans. The remains of the St. Albans theatre are particularly interesting. It had a wooden stage, dressing-rooms, and a semi-circle of tiered seats.

Amphitheatres were built outside towns. They were round, had banks of seats, and were open to the sky. A variety of spectacles took place there,

from boxing, cock-fighting and bear-baiting to public executions and gladiatorial contests, when slaves, criminals or prisoners of war were put into the arena to fight each other or wild animals.

There are no remains in Britain of circuses, which were like our sports tracks and where chariot racing took place, but we know from *mosaics*, sculptures and inscriptions found here, that they must have existed.

The Roman baths at Bath (Aquae Sulis). What you see above ground is a reconstruction of what the baths looked like nineteen hundred years ago.

TOWNS

The Baths

The public baths (*thermae*) were for men only. After undressing, bathers rubbed oil into their skin, and went to the *tepidarium*, the warm room, where they could laze in warm water. Next came the *caldarium*, the hot steamy room, where they bathed again and scraped their skin clean with a carved blade, called a strigil. After that came a swim in the cold pool, and to finish a massage with perfumes and oils. In the gardens of the thermae or in a nearby covered hall there might be wrestling, gymnastics or racing.

Water was heated by a furnace, and hot air from the furnace circulated under the floor, and up through ducts built in the walls. This under-floor heating area was called a *hypocaust*. If you can, visit the Roman baths at Bath.

A hypocaust, allowing the floor supported by these short pillars to be heated by the circulation of hot air.

THINGS TO DO

1 There is an excellent museum in Cirencester with models of Roman shops, workshops and the different rooms of a house. Try to go to see it. Credworth villa is also only a few miles away. Perhaps your local museum has Roman remains, too. You could also try to plan your own Roman town, or even perhaps build a model of it.
2 Here is a list of some Roman towns with their Latin names: York (Eboracum), Chester (Deva), Bath (Aquae Sulis), London (Londinium), Lincoln (Lindum), Leicester (Ratae). Can you identify these towns on the map?

CHECK YOUR UNDERSTANDING

Can you remember the meaning of the following words?

Aqueduct
Basilica
Forum
Hypocaust
Tabularium

CAN YOU REMEMBER ?

Colchester, Lincoln and Gloucester were built for the same purpose. What was it? The Romans usually built towns in a grid system. The squares that were formed were called insulae *(Latin for islands). Why was the basilica built in the middle of the town? Why were the barracks situated near the gates of a town? What happened at the amphitheatre?*

Agricola

The Roman historian Tacitus wrote a biography of his father-in-law Agricola, who became governor of Britain in 78 AD. This is what he wrote about Agricola's policy of encouraging the growth of towns.

> The following year (79–80 AD) was devoted to the most sensible policies. A people which is scattered and uncivilized is quick to fight. To make peace and leisure acceptable he had to show how pleasant they were, so he gave to both individuals and communities encouragement and official assistance to build temples, town centres and houses, with praise for cooperation, and rebuke for all who were reluctant. They competed to win his favour and compulsion was unnecessary. . . . Gradually, the Britons sank to the demoralizing pleasures to be found in the porticoes, bath-houses and elegant dinner-parties. These simple people called it 'civilisation'; really it was only one way of keeping them quiet.

> **(From Tacitus, *Agricola*)**

Amphitheatres

There were many amphitheatres. The best preserved is at Caerleon. It was built by legionaries, and was probably used as a parade-ground as well as for amusement. An inscription found there reads:

> From the tenth cohort, the century of Flavius Jolinus (built this).

Some other relics of amphitheatres that have been found are a gladiatorial bronze helmet at Bury St. Edmunds, a brooch at Lakenheath depicting a man fighting a lion, and pottery at Colchester with pictures of lions and a bear. Amphitheatres were commonly built using natural depressions or on neolithic monuments, and therefore used a minimum of timber in their construction. Because of this they are often the only buildings surviving above ground level, for example at Silchester and Cirencester.

We learn from this passage that it was advantageous to the Romans to build towns. What advantages might there be for the Britons to live in towns, rather than in the country?

The theatre at St. Albans, first built about the middle of the second century AD. The tall column standing on the stage has been rebuilt. The theatre was probably used for religious ceremonies as well as for staging plays.

Excavations tell us that for many people living in the country the coming of the Romans made little difference to their way of life. Most people continued to live in very simple houses, they worked very hard, and by our standards they had little leisure time and died young.

The Roman army, however, created a vast new market. It needed huge amounts of food, wool and leather, and British farmers were expected to supply them. The extent to which individual farmers prospered largely depended on how far they lived from a good road, or from a fort or a town, where they could sell their goods.

The Romans brought with them new farming techniques. Their ploughs were more efficient and they introduced a new kind of oven for drying grain more effectively, which meant that it could be stored for a much longer time. In addition they brought more land into production by draining marshes and fenland.

They also introduced new fruits and vegetables such as apples, cherries, plums, broadbeans and peas, and many herbs such as coriander, dill and oregano. The main crops were still wheat, barley and oats and some herbs were used as medicines as well as in cooking. Cows were kept chiefly for beef and leather, and sheep for meat and wool. In addition, chicken, ducks, goats and pigs were all reared at this time.

Certain areas of land the Romans took over for themselves. Their two largest estates were one near Salisbury, where they had about 2,500 square kilometres, and the other around the Wash, where they seized twice that area. We know that some tenants of these estates had to hand over to the army, either free of charge or at a fixed price, half of all the corn they grew.

Although life for most people in the country must have been exceedingly hard, there were clearly those who prospered, and who built on their farms houses which became increasingly large and luxurious. These were called *villas*, and most villas have been found in the south-east of England near towns, and along main roads. In the first century their design was simple: the original villa at Lockleys near St. Albans, for example, consisted of a

block of five or six rooms with a verandah in front. In the third and fourth centuries, when most villas were built, they became bigger and more ornate. Wings were added to the central block to create a courtyard, and many villas had underfloor heating called a *hypocaust*, suites of baths and even saunas. Chedworth in Gloucestershire is particularly well-preserved with beautiful mosaic floors, painted walls, and a temple in the garden. As well as living

accommodation villas had barns, granaries and stables for animals. At Sparsholt, a building almost certainly used for labourers living quarters' has been found. One of the biggest villas is at Woodchester in Gloucestershire. Crafts and industries were carried on in some villas. Lansdown villa above Bath produced pewter ware, and Park Street villa near St. Albans made roof tiles. Other villas produced glass and worked iron.

A country scene showing a shepherd looking after his flock – Strabo mentions corn as one reason for the Roman invasion, and later Britain was noted for its woollen goods throughout the Western empire.

COUNTRY LIFE

The Farmer's Wife

Lucius Columella, writing in the first century A.D. said:

> The master should build the best possible house, that is compatible with his financial resources, so that it may entice him not only to come to the country more willingly, but also to stay in it with greater pleasure. Especially is this the case, if he is accompanied by his wife. Her feelings, like those of all her sex, are more fastidious, and she will be honoured by some comfortable features to induce her to stay more happily with her husband. Let the farmer build elegantly, therefore.

Q

What does this passage tell us about Roman attitudes to women?

Hunting

A popular occupation among villa dwellers was hunting. Strabo noted that British hunting dogs were prized in other parts of the empire (the castorware pot on the right shows a hunting scene, a popular motif), and until recently there was a lively mosaic from a villa at East Coker in Somerset showing huntsmen on their way home with a deer slung between poles. One surviving inscription from another villa in Somerset reads:

> C. Indutius Felix, willingly and deservedly fulfilled his vow to Silvanus, for the deities of the deified emperors

This is a dedication to the god of hunting, Silvanus, which also indicates the extent of emperor worship within Roman Britain.

THINGS TO DO

1 Find out where your nearest Roman villa is, and ask your parents or your teacher if you can go to see it.

2 Why do archaeologists have to dig to find out about the past? An encyclopaedia will tell you the answer.

3 Many herbs used by the Romans still grow near Hadrian's Wall. Can you discover the names of some of the herbs and flowers that we use today for medicinal purposes, and the illnesses they help to cure?

Notice the size of these oil and wine jars. What do you think the oil might have been used for besides cooking?

A House in the Country

Pliny was a very successful lawyer and politician, and here is part of his description of his country villa in Italy.

> My house is on the lower slopes of a hill ... It faces mainly south and so from midday onwards in summer (a little earlier in winter) it seems to invite the sun into the colonnade ... Almost opposite the middle of the colonnade is a suite of rooms set slightly back and round a small court shaded by four plane trees. In the centre a fountain plays in a marble basin, watering the plane trees round it and the ground beneath them with its light spray ... There is also another room, green and shady from the nearest plane tree, which has walls decorated with marble up to the ceiling, and a fresco (which is no less attractive) of birds perched on the branches of trees.

(Pliny, *Letters*)

As well as its spray watering the plane trees, why would a fountain be an attractive feature of Pliny's villa?

CAN YOU REMEMBER ?

How can we tell that many people had hard lives and died young?
Why are good roads important for economic prosperity?
What fruits and vegetables did the Romans bring to Britain?
How was more land brought into production?
Why were many villas built in the south-east of England?

The relief below shows a Roman harvesting machine. The donkey was used to push the scoop into the corn.

CHECK YOUR UNDERSTANDING

Can you remember the meaning of the following words?

Appropriated
Excavations
Granaries
Ornate
Villas

GOVERNMENT

Britain is a democracy. If we do not like the government, we have the opportunity every five years to vote for a different political party, which may form a new government. Under the Romans, Britain was basically a dictatorship. Britons were allowed to choose members of certain councils that had limited powers, but when it came to matters of defence, finance, and the enforcement of the law, the Romans kept power firmly in the hands of officials appointed by the Imperial government.

The governor of a province was a Roman appointed by the emperor, and he was very powerful indeed. He was both commander-in-chief of the army, and the chief law officer. All cases involving either large sums of money or the death penalty were referred directly to him and he was appointed for not less than three years. Agricola, for example, served for six. By the fourth century the governor's workload had become so great that a special legal post, the *legatus iuridicus*, was created.

The *procurator* was another imperial appointment. His work was financial, and his main task the supervision of the collection of taxes. There were three main taxes: a land tax assessed on the value of animals and crops, a poll tax levied on individual's income and wealth, and the *annona*, the collection, probably at a controlled price, of corn and other goods for army use. There were also customs duties, death duties and a tax on setting slaves free.

For most of the occupation much of the countryside was under direct military rule. The northern frontier region was probably controlled by the head of the army in York, while large parts of Wales were ruled by military commanders at Caerleon and Chester, who as well as keeping the peace would be expected to settle disputes, collect taxes and maintain roads. In some tribal areas, for example those of the Iceni and the Atrebates, chieftains were expected to maintain order, but a Roman military presence was never far away.

In well-populated areas there was a greater degree of self-government. Many settlements ran their own affairs through two elected officials, and possibly a council. In larger centres, the ruling body was the *ordo*, a council with about a hundred members. At first, it was an elected assembly, but from the second century members were co-opted, that is, invited to join. Women were barred, and all members had to be at least thirty, have a certain degree of wealth and be freeborn. Magistrates appointed by the ordo were responsible for minor legal matters, the upkeep of public buildings including temples, the maintenance of roads, the supply of water and drainage, and the collection of local taxes. Being a magistrate was not popular, as they were often expected to supply some services out of their own pockets.

As well as the ordo, there was a provincial council composed of delegates from different regions. We know little about this council, except that it took responsibility for the worship of the emperor, and that its president was also the chief priest.

An artist's reconstruction of Roman Wroxeter, third century AD. Unlike country areas which were governed by the army, towns elected their own officials and magistrates who supervised local affairs and collected taxes for the Imperial government. Look at the hippodrome (race track for horses) on the right. What other features of the town can you see?

GOVERNMENT

A Good Governor

Here is Tacitus, a historian writing in about 100 AD, describing how his father-in-law Agricola fought against corruption.

Agricola knew how the provincials felt, and seeing from the experience of others that an unjust administration undid any success won by the army, he resolved to eradicate the causes of war. Beginning at home he first put his own staff in order; that task is as difficult for most people as governing a province ... He knew everything that happened, but often turned a blind eye. Small offences he pardoned, serious crimes he dealt with severely. Penitence satisfied him more often than penalties. He tried to appoint honest men to positions of responsibility to avoid having to punish the dishonest. He eased the burden of taxation by distributing it fairly, and cut out the profitable rackets, which the British objected to more bitterly than taxation!

(Tacitus in *Agricola*)

Roman citizens registering their names – being a Roman citizen brought special privileges in areas such as the law.

What does it mean to 'turn a blind eye'? Would you agree that this is sometimes a good idea?

Money

The main Roman coins were the bronze *as*, the silver *denarius* and the gold *aureus*. Julius Caesar began the tradition in Britain of showing the ruler's head on one side of the coin.

Why is it difficult to work out in the coinage of today what a Roman aureus was worth? If you find this question hard to answer, ask your parents or grandparents what they earned in their first jobs.

(Below) This coin shows a Roman galley (see p.14). (Right) A coin from the reign of Emperor Claudius 41–54 AD.

The Imperial Post

The Imperial Post carried military despatches and official messages and instructions throughout the empire along a vast network of roads and sea-routes. Without the post, emperors would have found it impossible to know quickly what was happening in the empire, and subsequently, how to maintain government. Couriers travelled, on horseback or in carriages, an average of fifty miles a day. The cost of the upkeep of roads mostly fell on local communities, who also paid for the *mutationes*, staging posts where horses could be changed, and *mansiones*, where overnight accommodation and stabling could be obtained. The mansio at Silchester was a very large one, presumably because Silchester lay on several routes. It had a big bath house, and several suites of rooms arranged around a courtyard. These suites of rooms were markedly larger and more luxurious than the rooms of private houses, and would seem to have been built for travellers of importance. Permits had to be obtained to use the post.

Letter from the writer Pliny the Younger to the Emperor Trajan:

Are permits to use the Imperial Post valid after their date has expired, and if so, for how long? . . . I am anxious not to make the mistake through ignorance of sanctioning illegal documents, or alternately of holding up essential dispatches.

Trajan's reply:

Permits to use the post must not be used once their date has expired. I, therefore, make it a strict rule that new permits are sent out to every province before the date they can be needed.

(Pliny, *Letters*)

Why do you think permits had to be obtained before you could use the Imperial Post?

THINGS TO DO

1 The governor of a Roman province was very powerful indeed. Can you find out what real power our monarchy still has? Britain is a democracy, because we can choose our government. How old do you have to be to be able to vote? Why is it important that at the polling station, when we vote, no-one can see whose name we put our tick beside?
2 Most city council meetings are open to the public. Ask your parents or your teacher if they will take you to one. They are usually very interesting.

CAN YOU REMEMBER ?

What powers did the governor of a Roman province have? For how long was he appointed? Can you name the chief taxes the British people had to pay? Who was responsible, amongst other things, for the upkeep of public buildings and the supply of water? Why was his job not one that many people wanted to have?

CHECK YOUR UNDERSTANDING

Can you remember the meaning of the following words?

Annona
Coopted
Magistrate
Ordo
Procurator

RELIGION

Religion was a very important part of Roman life. Romans believed that there were many gods, who controlled their destinies, and that when these gods were honoured, they brought prosperity and good fortune.

Most Romans houses had a special place where the family worshipped. Three family gods were Janus, the god of the doorway, Lar, the god of the house, and Vesta, the goddess of the household fire, who was offered food and drink at the beginning of a meal.

When the Romans came to Britain, gods were already being worshipped, many of them associated with rivers, springs and wells, such as Coventina, the water goddess. In general, the Romans were tolerant of other religions, and often Celtic and Roman gods were worshipped side by side, as were Sulis and Minerva at Bath. Some other Roman gods were Jupiter, the supreme god, Apollo, the sun god, and Mars, the god of war, a particular favourite of soldiers.

Temple of Mithras, the Persian god of the sun, at Carrawburgh, near Hadrian's Wall. The temple was built in 205 AD. How do you think we know this date?

Chi/Rho symbol (see page 31) on a third century fresco from Lullingstone villa in Kent.

The Romans also introduced emperor worship, largely as a means of encouraging loyalty. The centre of this in Britain was Colchester, where a large temple was built, dedicated to the Emperor Claudius.

Each temple was dedicated to a particular god. They were built in a variety of styles, though most of them were quite small. Priests worshipped in front of a statue of the god inside a room others were never allowed to enter. This room had a tiled or mosaic floor, and the walls might be decorated with paintings. In front was an open courtyard, where worshippers stood. At Wroxeter the shrine, the room where the priests performed their ceremonies, was built on a platform. Some temples were very ornate with pillars and statues, such as those at Bath and Colchester. We have from a site in Norfolk a crown and five circlets with adjustable headbands that was probably worn by priests. Animal sacrifices were made on special occasions.

Burials took place outside towns. The Romans believed that when people died they went across a river to an underworld, and so they placed a coin with the dead person to pay Charon, the ferryman. Many people were buried with valuable possessions. At York, for example, jewellery and a mirror were found in a lady's grave.

Some eastern religions spread to Britain and were accepted, the most important being the worship of Mithras, the Persian god of light, and Isis, the Egyptian mother goddess. Christians, however, were persecuted, mainly because they refused to take an oath of loyalty to the emperor, and the first Christian martyr in Britain, executed in 209, was St. Alban, who had served as a Roman soldier.

Gradually, though, Christianity spread, and after the Emperor Constantine made it a legal form of worship in 313 AD there is a good deal of evidence of Christianity in England. The Chi/Rho Christian symbol (see over the page) is found on many articles, Romano-British bishops attended a council of the whole church in Arles in France, and we know that there were Christian churches in the Roman towns of Silchester, St. Albans and Richborough.

RELIGION

The Druids

The Druids were Celtic priests, whom the Romans greatly feared because of their barbaric practices and power over the people. We know very little about what they did in Britain, but Tacitus describes the defenders of Anglesey like this:

> The enemy was arranged along the shore in a massive, dense and heavily armed line of battle... Women dressed in black like the fairies, were thrusting their way about in it, their hair let down and streaming, and they were brandishing flaming torches. Around the enemy host were Druids uttering prayers and curses, flinging their arms towards the sky. The Roman troops stopped short in their tracks, as if their limbs were paralysed... However, in the end exhortations from their commander... broke the spell. They overran those who resisted them and cast them into their own flames. Subsequently, a garrison was imposed on the defeated enemy, and the graves sacred to savage superstitions destroyed (these people regarded it as a right to sprinkle their altars with the blood of prisoners, and to consult the wishes of the gods by examining the entrails of humans).

> (From Tacitus, *Annals*)

Q

What sentence tells us, that although the Romans sometimes sacrificed animals in their temples, they were totally opposed to the sacrifice of humans?

CHECK YOUR UNDERSTANDING

Can you remember the meaning of the following words?

Circulet
Mosaic
Sacrifice
Shrine
Tolerate

CAN YOU REMEMBER ?

Who were the three family gods?
Why did the Romans encourage emperor worship?
Did the Romans accept religions, that they found in Britain? How do we know?
Why did burials take place outside towns? Why do you think valuable possessions were often buried with their owner?
What were the eastern religions that were accepted in Britain?

THINGS TO DO

1 St. Alban was the first Christian put to death in Britain because of his faith. He was a Roman soldier. Find out his story.
2 Can you discover the names of other Roman gods?
3 Some Christian festivals today actually had their origins in religions that existed before the Romans came – try to find out which they were and what pagan customs we still practise.

A statuette of a Romano-British god – evidence of Roman tolerance towards other religions.

Curses

Ghosts, black magic and curses were taken seriously in the Roman world. Here is a curse written on a piece of lead and found in London.

Fix Tertia Maria and her life and mind and memory and liver and lungs mixed, fate, thoughts, memory, so she may not be able to speak secrets.

Another curse, found in Gloucestershire, reads:

To the God Nodens: Silvianus has lost his ring. He has dedicated (its value) to Nodens. Among those who are called Senicianus, do not allow health until he brings it to the temple of Nodens.

What do you think 'fix' means here?

Pottery figurines found in a child's grave in Colchester, for use in the underworld.

Secret Messages

Here is a word square found scratched on a plaster wall in Cirencester. It reads the same in all four directions, and means 'Arepo the sower holds the wheels carefully'.

```
R O T A S
O P E R A
T E N E T
A R E P O
S A T O R
```

Rearrange these letters and you have

```
A               P               O
                A
                T
                E
                R
P A T E R N O S T E R
                O
                S
                T
                E
O               R               A
```

Pater Noster are the first two words of the Lord's Prayer in Latin; the extra O and A are Alpha and Omega, the first and last letters of the Greek alphabet.

The Christians were amongst the earliest people to adopt a logo. The first two letters of Christ in Greek are Chi, written as X, and Rho, written as P. These are placed one on the other to form the symbol below. This logo has been found in many places, scratched in silverware and tiles and carved in stone.

The lives of rich and poor in Roman Britain were very different. In the country most peasant houses were a single room, with walls made of interwoven branches packed with mud, and a thatched roof. Food was very monotonous, consisting mainly of a kind of porridge, or a rough bread. Vegetables such as cabbage, carrots, parsnips and celery were eaten, and meat, when it was available. The main garments for both men and women were tunics and cloaks. Everyone spoke Celtic, but increasingly most people would acquire some knowledge of spoken Latin. They worked on the land from childhood. Tombstones and graves tell us that many children died before they were five, and most people died before they were fifty.

The lives of rich people living in towns or country villas were very much more comfortable. Their houses, heated by hot air circulating beneath the floors, had separate kitchens, dining rooms,

The student shown in this mosaic is holding a stilus, *which he would use for writing by marking the surface of wax tablets.*

Romano-British peasants. Notice the contrast between their dress and that of the woman in the picture on p. 33.

bedrooms and bathrooms. They had tables, chairs and stools, but usually slept on the floor on mattresses with pillows and blankets. When they ate they lay on couches. Food was very varied, and wine, beer, ale or mead, made from fermented honey, were drunk. A first course might consist of oysters, other shellfish, snails or eggs. Fish was popular and was usually served in a sauce made from honey, wine and herbs. Meat, also, was often cooked in a highly flavoured sauce. Dessert could be fruit or cake. Archaeologists say that there is a marked increase in tooth decay in British graves of the Roman period.

A distinctively Roman garment for men was the *toga*, a piece of cloth about 6 metres long, folded across the body over the tunic. In Britain, it was probably only worn by wealthy men at important ceremonies. Over their tunics, which reached to the ground, women wore outdoors the *palla*, a large, rectangular piece of cloth, which, as they did not appear in public bareheaded, could be pulled over their hair.

A wide range of cosmetics was used. Foundation cream was made from the sweat of sheep's wool, chalk and white lead were used as powder, and red ochre as rouge. Powdered ashes darkened eyebrows, there were perfumes, and very elaborate hairstyles.

Girls were never given formal schooling, but for boys of rich families, education was very important indeed. They were taught either at home or in small groups. Reading and writing in Latin were the main subjects until the age of ten, and after that Latin grammar, literature, poetry, Roman history and philosophy. Children wrote on waxed wooden tablets with a *stilus*, a pen made of either bronze or iron, sharp at one end for writing, and blunt at the other for rubbing out. Letters and books were written in ink on parchment or papyrus, or sometimes on thin sheets of wood.

Physical fitness was a matter of great pride to men and boys, and running, wrestling and throwing the javelin were all popular sports.

A Roman woman surrounded by her attendants and looking at herself in a mirror.

Slavery

We know that there were slaves in Roman Britain. A tombstone found in South Shields has the inscription in Latin:

To the memory of Regina, of the Catuvellaunian tribe, who died aged 30, freed woman and wife of Barates of Palmyra, who set this up.

A letter on the wooden backing of a wax tablet found in London says,

Greetings to Epillicus and all his fellow slaves. I think you know that I am well. If you have made out a list, please send it. Keep a careful eye on everything, and turn that slave-girl into cash.

A large number of infant burials at the villa at Hambledon suggests that these were the children of slaves. There are other pieces of evidence of slavery, but the actual numbers of slaves, or their proportion to the rest of the population is very difficult for archaeologists to estimate. Some slaves were freed by their masters, or given freedom at their masters' death. Others were able to purchase freedom.

Q

What clues might tell archaeologists that the skeletons they are digging up are those of slaves?

CHECK YOUR UNDERSTANDING

Can you remember the meaning of the following words?

Cosmetics
Mead
Palla
Stilus
Toga

A carving (from Gaul) of either slaves or prisoners, chained by their necks.

Roman Numerals

1	I	9	IX	30	XXX
2	II	10	X	40	XL
3	III	11	XI	50	L
4	IV	12	XII	60	LX
5	V	13	XIII	90	XC
6	VI	14	XIV	100	C
7	VII	19	XIX	500	D
8	VIII	20	XX	1000	M

Can you work out what 88 and 234 would be in Roman numerals?

Roman numerals are still used today. Where have you seen them?

Education

As soon as a boy has learned to read and write without difficulty it is the turn of languages and literature . . . the art of speaking correctly and the art of interpreting the poets must be studied. The omission of philosophy is a drawback.

(From Quintillian, *Education of the Orator*)

This is a description of education, written by Quintillian, tutor at the court of the Emperor Domitian in the first century. It is very different from our ideas about education today.

If you could have introduced one subject into the Roman curriculum, what would it have been? Give reasons for your choice.

THINGS TO DO

1 We have refrigerators and freezers in which to keep our food. Can you find out how people hundreds of years ago tried to keep food through the winter? Why do you think the Romans cooked much of their meat and fish in highly flavoured sauces?

2 Below is a Roman dining scene – can you spot four main differences from a modern dining room?

3 Try to arrange a visit to the British Museum in London or a site such as Fishbourne near Chichester. Exhibits there will give an idea of what it was like to live in Roman Britain.

CAN YOU REMEMBER ?

What did people use to write? How were rich people's houses heated?
Can you name some of the sports that were played?
Ladies covered their hair when they appeared in public. How did they do this?
Archaeologists tell us that there was more tooth decay in skeletons dating from Roman times. What does this tell us about the diet at that time?

TRADE AND INDUSTRY

Under Roman rule there was a brisk trade between Britain and the continent. London was Britain's principal port, and archaeologists have found the remains of wharves stretching along 500 metres of the river Thames. Some other important ports were Richborough on the Kent coast, Dover, Hamworthy near Poole, Sea Mills near Bristol, Chester and York, which in Roman times could be reached by sea-going ships.

One of the chief imports into Britain was samian ware, red pottery made in Gaul. Pottery also came from the Rhineland, and clay lamps from Gaul, Italy and Africa. Good quality glass and metal work were also in demand. Wine arrived in large quantities, at first from Spain, Italy and Greece, but later from Gaul and the Rhine as well. Oil and olives were also imported, and some rather stranger commodities. An *amphora*, a large storage jar, found at Chesterholm was labelled 'prime mackerel sauce',

and another found at Carpow contained cough mixture for the army.

Less is known about British exports. We do know that British oysters were popular in Rome, and linen and woollen goods in Western Europe. Whitby jet was discovered in the Rhineland, and British woollen cloaks featured in a law of the Emperor Diocletian fixing prices.

Gold, silver, copper, lead, iron, tin and coal were all mined in Britain at this time. There was a large gold mine at Dolaucothi in South Wales, worked at a considerable depth largely by convicts and slaves.

Some Romano–British pottery. What might each dish or jug be used for?

A mosaic of a fishmonger. Can you find out what FELIX means?

A Roman glass beaker found at Mucking in Essex. It dates from about 400 AD. Precious objects such as these might well have been buried to hide them from invading Saxons and Franks (see also p. 40 and p. 43).

The use of salt in the preserving of meat and fish, and in the tanning of skins made it another important item in the British economy, and in the Emperor Diocletian's list of prices its value was assessed as the same as that of wheat.

Trade and industry could not have flourished as they did without the many roads that the Romans built. These roads were built primarily to carry military traffic, but they greatly facilitated the transport of goods. Three of the most important roads were Watling Street from Richborough near Dover to Wroxeter in central Wales, Ermine Street from London to York, and Fosse Way from south Devon to Lincoln. Main roads were 6 to 9 metres wide, and built as straight as possible, using local materials. Many older trackways, such as the Ridgeway, were improved by being widened, and gravelled.

The Romans also built canals in Britain, both for transport and for drainage. The river and canal system linking East Anglia and York was particularly extensive.

Most of the gold went to the emperor, but goldsmiths' shops have been found in York, St. Albans, London and Cirencester. Silver also went to the emperor, mainly for use in the minting of coins.

The manufacture of pottery was carried out on a very large scale. A wide range of pottery was used in every house for storage and cooking, and replacements were always needed. Most pottery was made in small local workshops, but Oxfordshire and the New Forest were two areas where large-scale production took place.

Roman Britain's Resources

Lead is used for the manufacture of pipes and thin sheets. In Spain and Gaul it is mined with difficulty, but in Britain there are such large quantities near the surface, that there is a law limiting its exploitation.

(From Pliny, *Natural History*)

The climate is wretched with its frequent rains and mists... The soil will produce good crops, except olives, vines and other plants, which usually grow in warmer lands. They are slow to ripen, though they shoot up quickly – both facts being due to the same cause, the extreme moistness of the soil and atmosphere. Britain yields gold, silver and other metals to make it worth conquering. Its seas, too, produce pearls, but they are of a dark bluish-grey colour.

(From Tacitus, *Agricola*)

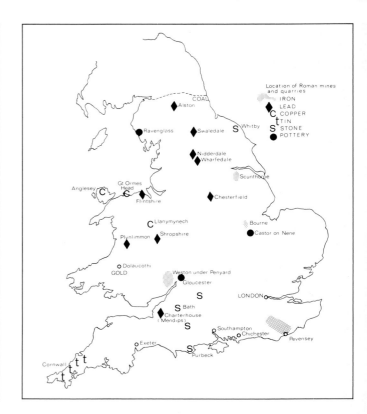

A map of industrial sites in Roman Britain.

Why do you think that Tacitus mentioned that vines and olives could not grow in Britain?

CAN YOU REMEMBER ?

How do we know that London was a very important port? Can you name some of the goods that were exported from Britain at this time? Why did the Romans build canals as well as roads? What metals were being mined in Britain?

THINGS TO DO

1 Draw a design for a wall painting.
2 Mosaic pictures can be made from a wide range of materials, including different kinds of paper and cloth, and even eggshell. See what you can do.
3 Many Roman roads were very straight. Find out if there is a modern road that follows the same route as a Roman road near you.

CHECK YOUR UNDERSTANDING

Can you remember the meaning of the following words?

Amphora
Commodities
Facilitated
Imports
Samian ware

Roman roads

The skilled surveyors and engineers of the legions designed and made a network of more than 10,000 kilometres of roads across the countryside (see map on p. 45). The foundations of the roads, approximately 1 metre below the surface, consisted of large rough stones. On top of this was a layer of smaller stones, often cemented together, and then a layer of gravel. Surface material varied according to what was available. Slag from iron mines, for example, made an extremely hard surface. Sometimes stone slabs were used, such as those at Blackstone Edge in the Pennines. Ditches were dug on both sides of the roads for drainage, and the slope from the centre of the road to the ditch might be as much as one in eight. We can tell from ruts in the roads that the standard width of Roman wagons was 1.4 metres. This is still the standard gauge of our railways today.

Two Crafts

Two of the more specialized crafts introduced by the Romans were mosaic making and wall painting. The first mosaic workshop was at Cirencester, and floors for public buildings, large town houses and villas were made there using chips of yellow and red brick, coloured glass, pottery, sandstone, slate and oolite to make the beautiful and complex pictures and patterns. Frescos, as some wall paintings are called, had to be painted while the plaster on the wall was still wet, the lime of the plaster bonding with the pigment of the paint. Other colours mixed with milk or the white of eggs, a process known as tempera, could then be painted on top.

Why do you think the Romans laid a level of gravel beneath the surface layer of their roads?

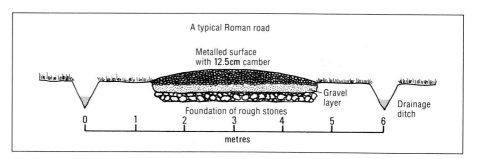

A typical Roman road

Metalled surface with **12.5cm** camber

Gravel layer

Foundation of rough stones

Drainage ditch

metres

How a Roman road was built.

A Roman road that still runs through Wheeldale Moor in Yorkshire.

By 410 AD the Roman army had left Britain, and the Emperor Honorius told the British that they must defend themselves. In the same year Rome itself was destroyed by the armies of Alaric the Goth.

For most of the period of Roman rule central Britain was a peaceful and prosperous place. Yet, for its size, Britain had a very large number of soldiers stationed there, and its frontiers were seldom safe.

First, there was the danger of attack by raiders from across the Irish and North Seas. From the beginning Roman ships were forced to patrol coastal waters, and in the third century the danger from Saxon invaders was so great that a chain of watch-towers and massive forts was built around the coast from Lancashire to East Anglia. Of these forts, Porchester, Pevensey and Richborough are particularly well-preserved.

The northern frontier was also difficult to maintain and we have seen how Hadrian's Wall and the Antonine Wall came to be built. At the end of the second century, after many of the forts and neighbouring villages along Hadrian's Wall had been destroyed by marauding tribes, the Emperor Severus divided the province of Britain into two, so that it could be more easily governed.

It was not only in Britain, however, that the Romans were threatened. During the third century the empire in central Europe was repeatedly attacked by barbarian armies. In addition, there were serious mutinies in the army itself, and by the middle of the third century the Roman garrison in Britain was being steadily weakened by the demand for troops to defend other provinces.

The first half of the fourth century was a prosperous one for Britain, but in 360 AD and again five years later bands of Picts and Scots attacked. Worse still, in 367 AD at the same time the Scots crossed the Irish Sea, the Picts attacked Hadrian's Wall, and the Saxons and the Franks invaded along the southern and eastern coasts. For a year Britain was ravaged, and it was only with great difficulty that the general Theodosius drove out the invaders.

From this time it became increasingly difficult for the Romans to maintain their hold of Britain. In 383 AD a British chief Maximus led a major revolt, and there were more Irish raids on the Welsh coast. The Romans were under pressure in Italy, too, where the armies of Alaric the Goth threatened Rome itself, and again regiments were taken from Britain.

The end came when a pretender emperor Constantine III took what was left of the Roman army in Britain to Gaul to establish his own power. In his absence in 408 AD the Saxons again attacked. Left defenceless, the British leaders appealed directly to the Emperor Honorius for protection. With Rome in ruins and his army heavily defeated there was nothing Honorius could do, and three hundred and fifty years of Roman rule in Britain were over.

The Great Dish from a hoard of fourth-century silver plate found at Mildenhall in Suffolk. How wealthy do you think the owners were?

Pevensey castle – this was a coastal fort built in the first half of the fourth century to defend Britain from attacks from the sea.

THE END OF ROMAN RULE

Troubled Times

Ammianus Marcellinus, writing at the end of the fourth century, tells us of the attacks on Britain in 360 AD.

> In Britain the savage tribes of the Picts and the Scots broke the treaties they had made: their raids and the devastation of the lands in the frontier region terrified the provincials, who were already exhausted by the series of present disasters.
>
> **(From Ammianus Marcellinus)**

The Emperor Valentinian was alarmed by serious news that the provinces of Britain had been brought to a desperate plight by a conspiracy of the barbarians: Nectaridus, Count of the Saxon Shore, had been killed, and the general Fullofauder had been caught in an ambush. The Roman general Theodosius restored peace in the end, but the following passage tells us that he had trouble not only with marauding tribesmen:

> In the end, by issuing proclamations and promising free pardons, he recalled the deserters to the standards, as well as many others scattered throughout the country on indefinite leave. At this summons most were induced to come back.
>
> **(From Ammianus Marcellinus)**

What does this tell us about the Roman army if, instead of a legion being decimated for cowardice, free pardons were given to deserters?

CAN YOU REMEMBER ?

What tells us that the Romans did not feel that their government in Britain was safe from attack?
How did the Emperor Severus tackle the problem of defence?
Why were Roman legions withdrawn from Britain?
What was one of the main reasons why the attacks on Britain in 367 AD were successful?

An Appeal to Rome

> And so a second time envoys set out with their complaints, their clothes (it is said) torn, their heads covered in dust, to beg help from the Romans. Like frightened chicks huddling under the wings of their faithful parents, they prayed that their wretched country should not be utterly wiped out.
>
> **(From Gildas, *The Ruin of Britain*)**

The Romans, however, were not inclined to help.

> The Roman standards, that great and splendid army, could not be worn out by land and sea for the sake of wandering thieves, who had no taste for war. Rather, the British should stand alone, get used to arms, fight bravely, and defend with all their powers their land, property, wives, children, and, more important, their life and liberty.
>
> **(From Gildas, *The Ruin of Britain*)**

Gildas, a British monk, wrote *The Ruin of Britain* in about 540 AD. It is a highly coloured account (he describes the Scots and Picts 'like dark throngs of worms, who wriggle out of narrow fissures in the rock'), but the one written nearest in time to the events he describes.

Treasure Trove

Largely because of the use of metal detectors, many more coins and other treasures are now found every year.

In November 1992 a very large hoard was found in Suffolk, consisting of about 1,000 gold coins, including some minted by the Emperor Honorius, fifteen gold bracelets, about 100 silver spoons (many bearing the Christian Chi/Rho symbol) and numerous other objects. The fact that the hoard contains coins of the Emperor Honorius suggests that, almost certainly, this treasure was hidden at the beginning of the fifth century to prevent it falling into the hands of raiders.

When gold or silver is found like this, the discovery has to be reported to an official, the coroner. If he decides that the owner buried it, he declares it a 'treasure trove' and forfeit to the Crown. In fact, it goes not to the Queen but to the British Museum, who gives the finder the market value of the objects. If the coroner decides that the treasure was lost by chance, it goes back to the finder or the owner of the land.

A hoard of Roman coins found at Bredgar in Kent.

What do you think might help the coroner to decide whether treasure was deliberately hidden or lost by chance?

CHECK YOUR UNDERSTANDING

Can you remember the meaning of the following words?

Marauding
Ravaged
Watch-towers

THINGS TO DO

1 Find out what you can about Alaric the Goth. Where did the Goths come from?
2 Hadrian's Wall was built to keep attackers out. A wall was built in Europe not long ago to keep people in. It was torn down in 1989. What was the name of this wall, and why was it erected?
3 Imagine you are a town official, afraid of attacks by Saxons. Write a letter to the Emperor explaining why you need support from Rome.

Table of Roman – Modern Placenames

Abona – Sea Mills
Alauna – Alchester
Anderitum – Pevensey
Aquae Sulis – Bath
Arbeia – South Shields
Branogenium – Leintwardine
Brocavum – Brougham
Burrium – Usk
Caesaromagus – Chelmsford
Calleva Atrebatum – Silchester
Camulodunum – Colchester
Clausentum – Bitterne
Coria – Inveresk
Corium Dobunnorum – Cirencester
Corstopitum – Corbridge

Deva – Chester
Durnovaria – Dorchester
Durovigutum – Godmanchester
Eboracum – York
Gabrosentum – Moresby
Glannoventa – Ravenglass
Glevum – Gloucester
Isca Dumniorum – Exeter
Isca – Caerleon
Isurium Brigantum – Aldborough
Letocetum – Wall
Lindinis – Ilchester
Lindum – Lincoln
Luguvallium – Carlisle
Magis – Piercebridge

Mamucium – Manchester
Moridunum – Carmarthen
Noviomagus – Chichester
Novus Portus – Dover
Petuaria – Brough-on-Humber
Portus Rutupiae – Richborough
Protus Lemanis – Lympne
Ratae Coritanorum – Leicester
Segontium – Caernarvon
Trimontium – Newstead
Venta Icenorum – Caistor-by-Norwich
Verulamium – St. Albans
Victoria – Inchtuthil
Viroconium Cornoviorum – Wroxeter

TIME CHART

BC 510   **Founding of Roman republic**
55   **Julius Caesar's 1st expedition to Britain**
54   **Julius Caesar's 2nd expedition to Britain**

AD 4   **Probable date of birth of Jesus Christ**
34   **Probable date of crucifixion of Jesus Christ**
43   **Invasion of Britain by Claudius. Britain became a Roman province**
43–84   **Conquest of Britain and Wales**
49   **Setting up of new town at Colchester for discharged legionaries and their families, beside the old settlement there**
60   **St. Albans established as thriving town**
61   **Rebellion of Iceni under Boudica. Sack of Colchester, London and St. Albans. Defeat of Boudica**
78   **Agricola made governor of Britain**
78–84   **Encouragement of growth of towns by Agricola**
90–98   **New towns established at Lincoln and at Gloucester**
122   **Building of Hadrian's Wall begun**
139   **Building of Antonine Wall begun**

150–160   **Rebellion in north crushed. Antonine wall temporarily evacuated, but reoccupied 158–163**
163   **Antonine Wall abandoned. Hadrian's Wall strengthened**
184   **Frontier fixed at Hadrian's Wall**
217–270   **Britain's most peaceful period under Roman rule**
222   **Goths and Vandals invade Roman Empire**
275   **Increase of Saxon raids on south-east coast. Most coastal forts built about this time**
313   **Christianity legalized by Emperor Constantine**
314   **Three British bishops attend Council of Arles**
367   **Britain invaded by Picts, Scots and Saxons**
369   **Order restored**
383   **More attacks by Picts and Saxons**
400   **Hadrian's Wall abandoned**
401   **Roman soldiers leave Britain to defend Italy**
408   **Probable Saxon invasion**
410   **Britons appeal to Emperor Honorius, but told to defend themselves without Roman help**
450   **Many towns in decline, and villas abandoned**
455   **Capture and sack of Rome by the Vandals, a tribe from North Africa**

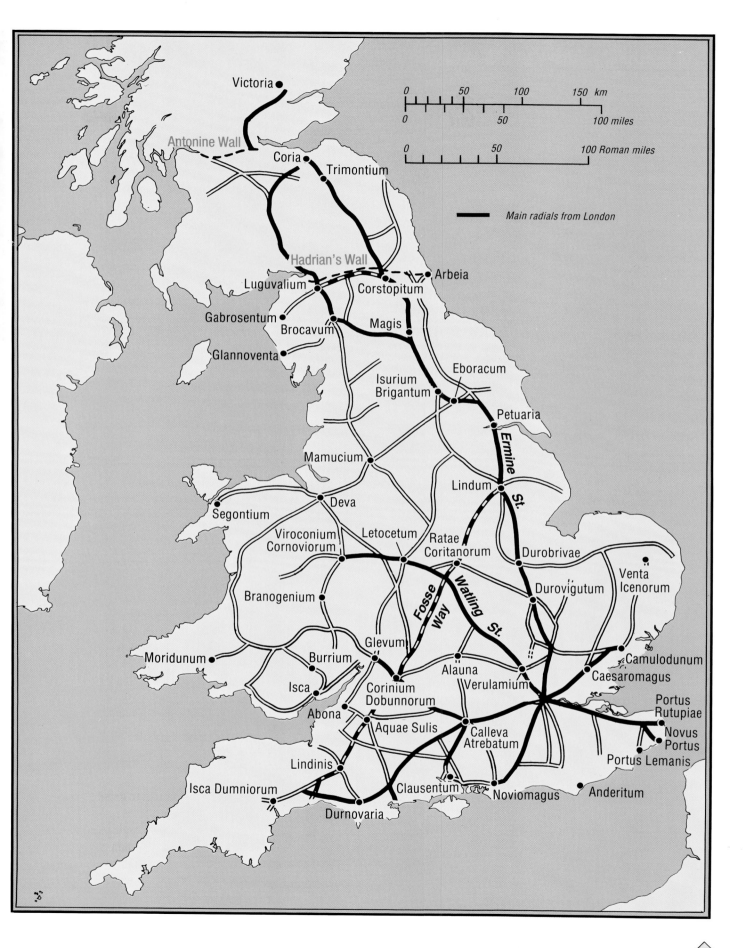

Victoria

Antonine Wall

Coria

Trimontium

Hadrian's Wall

Luguvalium
Gabrosentum
Brocavum
Glannoventa

Arbeia
Corstopitum
Magis

Isurium
Brigantum

Eboracum

Petuaria

Mamucium

Lindum

Deva

Segontium

Viroconium
Cornoviorum

Letocetum

Ratae
Coritanorum

Durobrivae

Venta
Icenorum

Branogenium

Durovigutum

Glevum

Alauna

Verulamium

Camulodunum

Caesaromagus

Moridunum

Burrium

Isca

Corinium
Dobunnorum

Abona

Aqua Sulis

Calleva
Atrebatum

Portus
Rutupiae

Novus
Portus

Portus Lemanis

Lindinis

Clausentum

Noviomagus

Anderitum

Isca Dumniorum

Durnovaria

Ermine St.

Fosse Way

Watling St.

——— Main radials from London

0   50   100   150 km
0   50   100 miles
0   50   100 Roman miles

GLOSSARY

Amphora   storage jar for liquids such as olive oil

Aquaduct   channel, usually above ground and built on stone or brick arches, for carrying water to a town

Auxiliaries   soldiers recruited from places in the empire other than Rome

Ballista   Very large crossbow, mounted on a cart

Basilica   Most important public building in a town. It contained the town hall and the law courts

Caldarium   The hot room at the baths with a pool of hot water

Centurion   army officer in charge of a century, which was usually eighty men

Cohort   six centuries of soldiers. Ten cohorts formed a legion

Decimate   put to death one man in ten

Forum   large open space in the middle of the town

Fresco   a water-colour painting on wall, done on damp mortar

Frigidarium   cold room at the baths with a cold pool

Garrison   soldiers stationed in a place for its defence

Gladiator   an armed man, usually a criminal, a slave or a prisoner of war, forced to fight to the death in the amphitheatre either another man or an animal

Greaves   below-the-knee armour to protect legs

Hypocaust   under-floor heating chamber. Hot air passed into the rooms above through ducts

Insula   one square or block of buildings in a town, built on a grid system

Legatos iuridicus   official in charge of legal affairs

Legion   largest division of the Roman Army, consisting of 4000–6000 men

Magistrate   elected governing official. The chief magistrates were called consuls

Mead   drink made from yeast, honey and water

Mosaic   picture or pattern made from small pieces of coloured stone or glass, cemented together

Onager   a very large catapult, which could hurl stones as far as 200 metres

Ordo   town council of about 100 members

Palla   woman's cloak

Papyrus   kind of paper made from reeds. They were dampened, pressed together and then dried

Parchment   writing material made from animal skins

Praetorian Guard   the emperor's body-guard

Procurator   officer, who collected taxes and paid soldiers

Quaestor   finance official

Rampart   mound of earth built up for defence

Shrine   special place in a house or temple, where people worshipped. Food and drink were often offered on shrines

Stilus   pen usually made from bone for writing on tablets. One end was sharp for writing. The other flattened for rubbing out

Tabularium   room where official records and documents were kept

Temple   place of worship, regarded as the home of the gods

Toga   garment worn by men, made from a large, circular piece of cloth

Tortoise   protection given by shields locked together over soldiers' heads

Tribute   tax paid every year by conquered people

Triumph   victory procession granted to a triumphant general

Villa   country house, usually quite large, part manor, part farm

What can you remember?

Which animal plays a part in the legend of the founding of Rome?

How long did Roman rule last in Britain?

When the Romans came to Britain, what goods did they hope to obtain?

Which emperor built the great wall that stretched right across the north of England?

We think of a circus as having clowns and acrobats and performing animals. What happened at the Roman circus?

Why did the presence of the Roman army mean that there was more trade between Britain and the rest of Europe?

Latin was the language the Romans brought to Britain. What language did ordinary people speak?

What did you have to have to be able to send a letter by the Imperial Post?

How do we know that an object found in a Roman excavation belonged to a Christian family?

What was a toga?

Name three Roman roads.

Who was the Roman emperor who told Britons that they must defend themselves?

FURTHER READING

For younger readers

Burrell R.E.C. and Peter Connolly, *The Romans*, Oxford University Press.

Peter Connelly, *The Roman Fort*, Oxford University Press.

M. Corbishley, *The Ancient World*, Hamlyn.

Anita Ganeri, *Focus on Romans*, Watts.

Rupert Mathews, *Roman Soldiers*, Wayland.

Hadyn Middleton, *Britons and Romans*, Simon & Schuster.

Jon Nicol, *The Greek and Roman World*, Blackwell.

Gillian Osband *Roman Britain*, (an Out and About activity book), National Trust.

Marjorie and C.B.H. Querrell, *Everyday Life in Roman Times*, Carousel.

Rosemary Sutcliffe, *The Silver Branch*, Puffin.

For older readers

John Clare, *Roman Empire*, (I was there Series), Bodley Head.

R.J. Cootes and L.E. Snellgrove, *The Ancient World*, Longman.

Anthony Marks and Graham Tingay, *The Romans*, Usborne Illustrated World History.

Peter Salway, *Roman Britain*, Oxford University Press.

Places to visit

There are many smaller local museums with Roman exhibits, but the following sites and museums are especially worth a visit: Roman Army Museum, Greenhead, Northumbria; Verulamium museum and theatre, St. Albans, Hertfordshire; Fishbourne palace and museum, Chichester, West Sussex; Roman lighthouse, Dover, Kent; Lullingstone villa, Sevenoaks, Kent; Roman baths, Bath, Avon; British Museum, London; Cirencester museum and Chedworth villa, Cirencester, Gloucestershire; Hadrian's Wall at Housesteads or Vindolanda, Northumbria; and Caerleon museum and amphitheatre, Gwent.

Acknowledgements

The Author and Publishers would like to thank the following for their kind permission to reproduce illustrations: Erich Lessing for pages 1, 15, 20–21 and 33; the Museum of London for pages 3 and 35; Ronald Sheriden Art & Architecture Collection for pages 5, 7, 9, 14, 19, 22, 23 (bottom), 26 (all three), 28, 29, 30, 32 (top and bottom), 34, 36, 37 (left and right), 40, 41 and 43; the Royal Commission for Historical Monuments for page 6; Peter Clayton for pages 12–13 and 18; the Castle Museum, Shrewsbury for page 24–25; and finally Ken Smith (illustrator) for the maps on pages 4 and 45 and the diagram on page 39.

INDEX